D1251682

The Challenge to
American Foreign Policy

JOHN J. McCLOY

Former United States High Commissioner for Germany

Harvard University Press, Cambridge, Massachusetts, 1953

DISTRIBUTED IN GREAT BRITAIN BY

Geoffrey Cumberlege

OXFORD UNIVERSITY PRESS

LONDON

LIBRARY OF CONGRESS CATALOG CARD NUMBER 53–8020
PRINTED IN THE UNITED STATES OF AMERICA

The Challenge to American Foreign Policy

The Godkin Lectures at Harvard University, 1953

EDWIN LAWRENCE GODKIN
1831–1902

Edwin Lawrence Godkin, editor of *The Nation* and the New York *Evening Post,* was born in Ireland of English stock, and took his degree at Queen's College, Belfast, in 1851. He published a *History of Hungary* and was associated with the London *Daily News* and the Belfast *Northern Whig* before coming to America in 1856. Here his letters to the *Daily News* on American public affairs attracted attention and prepared him for the task he assumed in 1865 as first editor of *The Nation,* to which he gave a scholarly quality, a breadth of view, and a moral tone that brought it recognition as one of the best weeklies in the English-speaking world. In 1881 *The Nation* became the weekly edition of the New York *Evening Post* of which Godkin was made editor in chief in 1883. From that time until his retirement in 1900 he exercised an influence on public opinion out of all proportion to the circulation of his paper. Editors throughout the country, whether in sympathy with his views or not, watched for his editorials on all important issues. He was exceptionally well read in economics, history and political theory, believed wholeheartedly in democracy, owed allegiance to no person or party, and was vigorous and fearless in expression. In 1903, by a gift to Harvard University, his friends established "The Godkin Lectures on the Essentials of Free Government and the Duties of the Citizen" in appreciation of his long and disinterested service to the country of his adoption and in the hope of stimulating that spirit of independent thought and devotion to the public service which characterized his career.

Foreword

In this book I have attempted to discuss a few of the problems facing the United States and the making and executing of foreign policy to meet them. It is difficult to point to a period in world history where the challenge to free men has been so widespread and so serious as in the present time. The heavy obligation rests upon all citizens of imagination and responsibility to study these problems and to try to find solutions. What follows is one citizen's attempt to derive from his experiences material or impressions of possible value to those whose duty it is to formulate and carry out our national policy.

In assembling my material I have drawn upon personal experience rather than upon research. In July 1952 I completed eleven years of almost continuous government or quasi-government service, most of it in a period of war emergency or sustained tension. My activities have been in the field of defense, of economics, and of foreign affairs.

In the latter part of 1952 I was connected with the Ford Foundation working on a project called "Conditions of Peace." I am indebted to the Foundation for the time it gave me to put together my impressions and thoughts for the Godkin Lectures at Harvard which provided the basis of this book.

JOHN J. McCLOY

April 17, 1953

Contents

The Challenge to American Foreign Policy

1

The Problems We Face

One hundred years ago, in his *Democracy in America*, Alexis de Tocqueville wrote:

There are on earth today two great peoples who from different starting points seem to move toward the same goal: the Russians and the Americans. Both have expanded in the shade. While the eyes of men were busy elsewhere, they have taken their place suddenly in the forefront of the nations, and the world has become aware, almost at the same moment, of their birth and of their greatness.

All other nations seem to have nearly reached their natural limits, and can only hold their own. These two nations are developing and expanding. All the others have stopped still or only advance slightly through great effort. These two stride forward easily toward a boundless destiny.

To achieve its objective, *America* relies on personal interest, and gives full and free reign to the strength and reason of the individual. *Russia* centers all the authority of society in a single man. The principal instrument of the former is freedom, of the latter slavery.

Their points of departure are different, they follow different paths. Nonetheless, each of them seems intended through some secret design of Providence to hold in its hands the destinies of half the world.

Today we face the problems inherent in the prediction Tocqueville so truly made. It will be our task for many years to come to discern the meaning of the fact that there are two colossi in the world: the one, as Tocqueville said, free, the other slave. This situation prevails at a time when we and all free peoples crave one major objective, and that is an honorable peace.

We seek peace, yet we feel that the Soviet colossus, despite occasional "peace" offers, poses a long-range threat to all free nations. Certainly, there is a dangerous imbalance in the world. It is important to analyze the full implications of this situation if we are to develop policies which will help restore a tolerable equilibrium. In this analysis, it is essential to cover (1) the real nature of the Soviet threat; (2) the requirements that must be filled to meet it; (3) the difficulties in the way of sound solutions; and (4) the political philosophy which should guide those solutions.

First, then, we should ask what is the real nature and emphasis of the Soviet threat — political, military, ideological or psychological?

The Soviet political threat stems directly from Soviet principles: the end — world domination by the ruling Soviet authority — justifies the means; the state is all and force is the fundamental tool of political power. Force holds the Soviet Union together. In Korea and

Czechoslovakia force is applied by resorting to aggressive war or to the gallows. In other countries under Communist control force casts a blight on every area of life. The normal day-to-day application of this force can best be seen in East Berlin or along the eastern boundaries of the German Federal Republic.

Behind the façade of Stalinallee in East Berlin, where huge structures are being built in the old tradition of dictatorships, are the grim faces of people badly clothed, living in danger and in fear. The hand and the spirit of the secret police are everywhere reflected in a grey and silent mood. Likewise, if one moves along the eastern boundaries of the German Federal Republic all the paraphernalia of the police state is painfully apparent — the barbed wire, the police dogs, the machine gun posts, the evacuated areas, the plowed-up strips, the nervousness and fears of thousands of refugees. They are all there and they are vital to an understanding of the Soviet threat.

These are the fundamental political elements of the Soviet threat. It is in the nature of the Soviet political drive that purge will follow purge and we would make a major mistake if we assumed that pacifists, humanitarians or liberals will appear at the Kremlin to change it.

This Soviet political drive is aggravated by the second aspect of the Soviet threat — the military. The Soviet Empire today has a great military preponderance in the number of men in uniform, in divisions and in equipment. All indications point to the fact that Soviet force, together with the forces of the satellites, is increasing. Contrary to the general impression in the free world, the gap between Soviet military power and the readily available military strength of the West is growing greater rather than less. This military threat is sharpened by the incontrovertible fact that Soviet forces are now supplied with the atomic weapon. Soviet political-moral concepts are such that the Kremlin would not be deterred from employing these atomic weapons. The terrible fact cannot be ignored that the Kremlin might use them, for example, in a sneak, Pearl Harbor-like attack.

Side by side with the political and military threat is the ideological, based on a doctrine which too few in the Free World comprehend. This ideology has made strong inroads wherever people have not been able to see what it really means in fact — the police state. The people of Free Berlin are immune to the ideology because they see it in action in East Berlin. The peoples of Czechoslovakia, Poland, East Germany and the other satellite states know what this ideology really means, but they do not have the power to overthrow the regimes which control them. However, in France, in Italy and in the other countries where freedom prevails, there are many who still firmly believe in the Communist creed.

The Kremlin knows the value of the ideological weapon and how to use it as a threat. The Soviets put great emphasis on the ideological attack. One example of this was Stalin's admonition, a few months before he died, that it was time for the Communists to produce a new book to be disseminated throughout the world. This need for and the emphasis upon the logos, which the Communists always display, is intriguing. There must be prepared a 500-page illustrated textbook, said Stalin, to supply the new unquestioned dogma, and 20,000,000 copies must be printed and distributed. The power of those 20,000,000 volumes should not be underestimated.

It is becoming more apparent each day that the Soviet is now combining all these threats to carry out a far-reaching policy of division among the free peoples of the world. It is this divisive technique which today poses the chief Soviet threat to the free world. It is here that the Soviets demonstrate their talent for destructive policy and it is here that we reach the central fact of the Soviet effort. The policy is division and the technique is ingeniously divisive both within nations and among nations. Every available device in every part of the globe is used to split apart the non-Communist world. Thus it is that every attempt which is made within a country to unite or among countries to effect a community of interest immediately prompts an intensive counter agitation on the part of the Soviets. Wherever the Communists find natural or artificial divisions they act rapidly to accentuate and encourage them.

This divisive technique is elastic. The Kremlin does not hesitate to ignore or contradict Communist ideology if, thereby, it is in a better position to divide. In Europe and in the Far East, it is spreading the poison of anti-Americanism in order to weaken efforts to coöperate with the United States. In France, old and well-grounded fears of Germany are stimulated and exploited. In Germany hostility toward France is generated to stifle the development of Franco-German partnership in the European community. The Neo-Nazis of Germany and the Arabs are urged to establish kinship with the Kremlin and enmity toward the free world. And the Soviets do not hesitate to throw in the note of anti-Semitism in order to promote these objectives. The technique recognizes no moral boundary or ideological consistencies. Fascism and even capitalism are embraced if by doing so division will be induced "Friendly" and hostile gestures are alternated in the effort to confuse the free nations.

Such is the many-sided nature of the Soviet threat. It operates everywhere, on all levels, with every weapon. To meet this threat heavy demands in energy, determination and imagination are placed on the free world, no less on the people of Europe than on the people of the United States. That brings us to the second major point — the requirements that must be filled to meet the threat.

The main counters to the Soviet threat are: the establishment of the unity of the free world which the Soviets are seeking with all means to prevent; the strengthening of our military forces; the maintenance of economic stability and, above all, the development among free peoples of stable attitudes and firm adherence to the unchanging goal of peace and freedom in the world.

Stronger unity of the free peoples is the fundamental element in successfully meeting the Soviet challenge. A combination of the political, economic and military potential of the free world would be more than a match for the Soviet onslaught. The development of a stronger United Nations, of the European community, of the North Atlantic Treaty Organization, of closer contacts among the uncommitted free nations of the Near, Middle and Far East would frustrate the Soviet divisive attack. The question is, therefore, whether the free world has the foresight, energy and will to accomplish this community of interest.

Along with the urgency for political unity is the need for increased military strength. The free peoples must prepare themselves militarily against sudden and outright attack. During the past two years, under the pressure of Soviet aggressions, some starts have been made toward increasing the military strength of the West. Yet the slightest relief from immediate anxiety has unfortunately created a tendency among free peoples

7

to slacken off preparation. Unless this habit is overcome the free world will not succeed in building up the solid military strength which is necessary to establish a balance and a true sense of security on which political stability can be maintained.

Before we turn from the question of military preparations it is essential to touch upon one matter of outstanding importance. It is the implication of atomic power in the hands of a totalitarian state.

The Kremlin is—or soon will be—capable of staging a sneak atomic attack. It does not seem possible that the United States or any democracy whose support depends on public opinion could employ such a tactic. This is a deeply important factor in our security considerations. The use of atomic power is of such crucial significance that it raises another basic question: should not more information be given to the people of the United States, if not of the atomic weapons themselves, at least of the implications of atomic development in this country and in Soviet Russia?

The question whether we have an adequate defense as well as an offense against the Soviet atomic threat needs prompt appraisal and decisions. We are approaching a situation where the Soviet potential might embody a knockout atomic blow even though our own atomic stockpile far exceeds theirs. If we do not have adequate defense, and I think it is quite obvious we do not now possess it, we shall have to find out whether it is possible to erect such a defense considering the heavy added burden it would represent on top of our present swollen tax structure. This is an urgent question in the field of our military preparation and like many questions of military preparation it involves far-reaching economic and perhaps social implications.

It is not necessary to emphasize the point that economic stability is required in the free world to strengthen our own unity and to counter Soviet divisive tactics. It is essential to make plans for a healthy exchange of goods and development of markets among all free nations irrespective of armament needs. Late in 1952 the Kremlin warned us of its interest in the economic field. Stalin gave us a most interesting exposition of his theory of economic dissension in the West. He confidently predicted that division among the non-Communist nations would grow as Germany and Japan seek to extend their markets. Moreover, he pointed out that these rivalries will become more embittered when the vast Communist countries, such as Russia and China, which were once export markets for the western nations and are now closed to them, begin to dispose of some of their surpluses in the few remaining markets of the West.

The political, military and economic counters are vital but it is increasingly apparent that the psychological must also be dealt with. It is essential that our mental attitudes be steadied so as to enable us to recognize and balance the various elements of the Soviet threat. Without it we cannot hope to avoid the discouragements which on the one hand lead to a relaxation of effort and on the other to the hysteria which produces unnecessary crises and shortsighted action. In brief, our public opinion must always be realistically attuned to the dangers, and unafraid to support flexible and positive policies and action. More specifically, the American people, while ready to continue their present sacrifices and, if necessary, to increase them, must have the poise which would permit our government to take advantage of any true Soviet move to reach a settlement on concrete issues, however broad their implications.

There are many imponderables in the areas and among the peoples that constitute the Soviet Union and its satellites. Within that vast mass many tensions and cleavages can and certainly will develop. If we were to adopt the Kremlin technique, we could deliver a manifesto ourselves foretelling the direful clash which will one day shake the Soviet regime, but there are more positive things for us to do and say. In spite of the ruthless character of Soviet policy, we must never lose sight of the possibility that progress toward a more rational relationship may develop if the Soviets are faced with the realization that their aims are no longer realistic. We should not rule out the possibility of discussing at an appropriate — though it now seems far distant — time a total disarmament scheme such as Grenville Clark proposes. This psychological factor must be emphasized because lack of balance has caused some of our past failures and might well interfere with our future success.

There is another important aspect to the problem of countering the Soviet threat with psychological and ideological tools. It is concerned with our ignorance of the Communist doctrine. Americans, with a few notable exceptions, really know little about that doctrine. Few know how to identify the difference between Communist theory and Communist practice. If it is wise to know your opponent, our leaders as well as our people have far to go to reach that point of wisdom. But reach it we must.

Such is the nature of the Soviet threat and some of the means to counter it. This leads to the third major point — the consideration of the difficulties, present and potential, which must be faced in finding the counter to the Communist challenge. These difficulties and problems exist throughout the world, in Europe, in Asia, and here at home. And in large part they are intensified by the Soviet divisive attack.

The major difficulty grows from the fact that the United States has power and that power brings with it leadership. No other nation or group of nations has emerged capable of exerting similar force in the modern power complex. But it is obvious that peoples with long histories and traditions are not likely to be enthusiastic about the leadership of a young, strong and rather volatile nation. No nation is comfortable in a position where it depends on another nation for economic support and for military defense. The Romans, the British, the French, the Spaniards, the Dutch, all had their day of preëminence and, irrespective of the manner in which they carried out their responsibility, the less powerful nations were never very happy about it. Those in a similar position are not happy today.

The nation which bears the responsibility of power must endure widespread misunderstanding and misrepresentation. It comes as a shock to Americans when from time to time our friends, whom we are sincerely endeavoring to assist, seem quite genuinely to be most irritated with us. They frequently display little sensibility to the enormous burdens we have so suddenly assumed or have had thrust upon us, and we dislike their tempers as sharply as they do ours.

In Europe, it has become increasingly apparent that our aid, though life-giving and welcome, has not uniformly endeared us to our allies. Indeed, the growth of anti-American feeling has assumed in certain quarters dangerous proportions. It is being expressed among the masses as well as among the intelligentsia. Those who condemn America's potential isolation are at the same time irked by American intervention. When we follow our traditional role of sympathy toward the unliberated, we stir bitterness in the metropolitan areas without any compensating friendship among the colonials.

We know that this irritation is stirred in great part by

the incessant Communist stream of anti-American poison, a poison which is injected into the life of every European, South American, and Eastern country. But though this stream may be the fundamental source of anti-American attitudes, the feeling is none the less there and must be reckoned with. We cannot ignore it, for it strengthens those divisive forces which would destroy first our friends and then ourselves.

The Communists are assisted in their campaign to divide the free nations by our unfamiliarity with foreign customs and sensibilities, by the element of jealousy among proud nations formerly dominant in world affairs, and by minor irritations such as the presence of our highly paid troops in communities and localities poorly equipped to absorb them. Our policy of urging greater participation by the European nations in the common defense program has also aroused resentments. Moreover, the aid programs themselves, though unparalleled in history, do not dispel this irritation. Europeans quite naturally do not like to hear once a year, during the period of the Congressional hearings on foreign aid, that they are beggars, that they do not work hard enough, and that they are not grateful enough. In the European mind these criticisms sometimes obscure the fact that, year after year, more positive voices in this country have carried the day for the continuation of the programs.

The problems and difficulties we face in Europe are

extensive. If we look to Asia, Africa and South America we see that the problems are enormous in scope and implication. It is vital that we recognize and try to meet those problems today instead of waiting to be engulfed by them ten years from now. It is essential, therefore, for us to pay increased attention to the non-European areas of the world, without for a moment losing our interest in Europe.

In India, in Pakistan, in areas that stretch from the Far East to the Middle and Near East, and in Africa, complex movements and stirrings are now taking place. The Hindu, Moslem and Buddhist masses are making known their wants. Their first need is concerned with elementary things: food, garments, housing. But it would be a mistake to conclude that these peoples any more than those with higher living standards can be satisfied merely with more things. Somehow, these peoples must arrive at the conviction that the Western nations are prepared to approach and deal with them in a spirit of coöperation and justice. That is easy to say and very difficult to accomplish.

The United States has already made substantial contributions to a solution of the problem of the underdeveloped areas. The Point Four Program, the lending activities of the Export-Import Bank and of the World Bank, which is heavily supported by the United States, the work of private foundations, the investments of American business, the support of private American organizations and groups have all been noteworthy. But in terms of the need, the work done has been small and we can be quite certain that aid is not the full answer. It is conceivable, for example, that the more we do to aid peoples in the East, the more competitive and perhaps antagonistic they may become toward other nations. We can be quite certain that there is no guarantee of lasting good will through gratitude for aid or relief. Nevertheless, the need to act in respect of these areas of the world is urgent. Apart from any humanitarian impulse, which is sufficient in itself, the condition of these areas is such that outside forces are bound to play heavily upon them. As in other areas of the world, the Kremlin is not only poised but also active in its effort to influence Asia against the Western democracies.

The problem is to convince the people of these areas, in spite of the divisive propaganda of the Soviets, that the Western democracies are sincerely desirous of coöperating with them in their struggle for better living conditions. For unless they have the conviction of our coöperation and unless there is some counteraction to the incessant Soviet penetration, the chances are that the nations of Asia will embrace Communism or be embraced by it. Once that has happened, all the regrets of the victims, all the recognition of Soviet failures and oppressions, are not going to restore the situation to what it was before the take-over. Studies more profound than any now available must be made in regard to the economics involved in this problem. Studies alone are not going to solve it, but we should know more than we do now about the relation of trade and aid. The problem is, of course, all bound up with the old familiars of the dollar gap, of investment needs, and of tariffs.

In considering these complex problems, we would all agree that Americans know little of the East, of its people, its religions, its policies and philosophies. We are vaguely aware that vast populations do live there but it is well to restate the figures: India, Pakistan and Burma, 450 million; Indonesia, 79 million; China, 464 million; Africa to the Cape of Good Hope, 198 million; all together, one-half of the population of the world.

These are figures with enormous implications. It cannot be a matter of indifference to the United States or to Europe what direction these great masses take in the next few decades. Where will they be by the year 2000, only forty-seven years away? They all have a long history, far longer than ours, but the mighty stream of their history is converging upon our own, as certainly as the rising and setting of the sun. What do we know about Hinduism, Islam or Buddhism, all of which are now seeking a rebirth, or of the other religions which move these great populations? What scanty means of communication and contact we now have with them, yet how deeply they may affect our future.

There is one problem of communication of particular interest here. Many of the present leaders of India,

Pakistan, Burma and other countries received their education in the liberal atmosphere of Oxford, Cambridge, London, and to a substantial degree at Harvard and at other great American centers of learning. They now know what a free society means. With the next generation of leaders in those countries we may find an attenuation of this contact. Apart from the difficulty many will have in obtaining dollars and pounds to study abroad, the new generation may well desire to stay at home and be trained in institutions of their own countries. They may even study in Russia. Such a change could have large implications in the years ahead for the attitudes and policies of the Eastern nations. This suggests the need for positive action in this country to make it possible for more Asiatics to study at our institutions as well as the need to support the Asiatic countries in developing their own training schools. We must keep open the channels of understanding. Our institutions must be made available to the future leaders of the East if we are to avoid unpleasant developments tomorrow. All in all, there is great need for a major resurvey of the measures we should take to bring the peoples of the East into closer political and economic association with the United States and the free peoples of Europe.

Asia is probably closer to the immediate stream of history than Africa. If we are to feel Asia's importance tomorrow, we may be finding the importance of Africa the day after tomorrow. The lands and peoples from

South Africa north to Egypt vary as the bands of the spectrum. They offer tempting targets to the Communists. Already Communist cells in some of the African countries are planning deeper penetrations. Where are the future leaders of Africa being trained? It is important that they, like the leaders of Asia, should not be trained in Moscow or under its influence.

Such are some of the difficulties we face abroad in meeting the Soviet threat. In meeting that threat we are confronted with serious problems at home. Along with the readily recognizable difficulties before us, the American people face a somewhat intangible threat that is perhaps the most sinister of all — and that is the threat to ourselves. With their emphasis on division, the Soviets have been successful in making us fear each other, or at least we are growing deeply suspicious of one another. We do not trust our neighbors and very few of our public officials. Yet it is faith and trust in each other that has always made America strong in decision and resolute in action.

This is not a call for a policy of make-believe. The discovery that a number of Americans have been willing to commit high treason; to be spies; to use high government office for the purposes of the Kremlin, has come as a great shock to our society, as similar action on the part of British citizens has shocked the Canadians and English. The fact that a few of our fellow citizens have been traitors is appalling. It means that there can be no let-up in sensible efforts to uncover those who work against us for Communist purposes.

But we cannot afford to lose perspective in the campaign to protect ourselves against agents and spies. We must not confuse men and women of liberal outlook with these activists. Nor must we permit our opposition to Soviet Communism to interfere with the careful consideration by our policy-makers of productive contacts with the Soviet government.

It is essential that an atmosphere of open discussion and of free debate should prevail in this country. It is important that we adhere firmly to the American principles of justice before the law. It is time we developed a method of protecting the community interest consistent with individual rights in a manner less spectacular and less political than the pressures of the last few years. Canada had an exposure just as shocking to its people as ours have been to us, but the matter was handled with a dispatch which it ought not to be too difficult to emulate.

Our posture at home is a matter of great concern to the world. Many peoples — the British, the French, the Germans, the Indians and others — do not question the fact that we hold a position of leadership. Many believe us unselfish in our aid and generous in our dealings. Despite widespread anti-American attitudes, there still exists in the world a great repository of good will toward this country. There is still a belief that America is a land of opportunity and of hope.

The peoples abroad know that we have power and good intentions. However, there is one big question in their minds. They wonder if our direction and our leadership will be sound. Much of this concern flows from the European and Asian attitude toward the question of war.

Although the possibilities of atomic warfare are such that all nations are open to destructive attack, Europeans, owing to their geographical proximity to Russia, feel that they are dangerously exposed to Communist aggression. Their recent past is full of the horrors of war. This knowledge and experience does not, as some would expect, take the form of a vigorous and determined attitude toward future aggression. Europeans are convinced that another war and occupation by a ruthless enemy, even if followed by reliberation, would mean complete loss of their civilization, so complete that it could not be rehabilitated. Europe, exhausted and weary, simply cannot accept the idea of war. It fears that the United States can.

This psychology produces a wide range of contradictions, highly comforting to the Communists. Our European allies, though they concede that they must rearm, are hesitant to move vigorously for fear of provoking the Kremlin. Though they were prepared to condemn the United States out of hand, had we not taken a stand on Korea, Europeans did not wish us to accept a real gauge of battle there. Unsure of the pose they themselves should assume, they charge that we will not strike the right balance between boldness and caution. Standing among the ruins of their own political history, the leaders of Europe fear that we are not as wise as they in statecraft. Yet they recognize that without our resolution, and in a certain sense, without our combativeness, the line of freedom would not be drawn as far forward as it is in the world today. The people of Europe recognize that the Berlin airlift and the repulse of aggression in Korea have had deep and positive consequences for the free world, but still they worry about our future conduct.

It is this mixture of strong reliance upon our protection and fear of our immaturity which has so much to do with the critical skein that runs through the thinking of the people whom we would befriend. As a result, we face the problem of reappraising what the other free nations can do and what we must do so that all of us will contribute our honest share of work toward the common goal.

*   *   *   *   *

In this chapter the complex, divisive and dangerous nature of the Soviet threat has been described. Some of the things we must do if we are to meet that threat have been indicated. Moreover, the attempt has been made to sketch the areas of difficulty which are ahead and which will demand mature judgment on our part if we are to have a reasonable chance of peaceful solutions to our problems.

The nature of the problems we face is such that the only solution to them appears to be a strong policy of unity. Even if the United States alone had the power to bring about a solution it would not be wise to do so. The multiple character of the problems posed by the Soviet threat can be met adequately only by a community of free nations working together. We may be the strongest element in that community, but we must work within it. It is essential for this country to find a way to exercise our proper influence, as a partner in a partnership and not as the leader telling others what to do.

There are many indications that the community chapter in history must now open. Economically and politically, the individual European nations do not hold the relative strength as against the rest of the world that once was theirs. Professor Toynbee may be going too far when he indicates that the European nations are now in the same relative status as the old city-states of Nuremberg, Genoa and Venice after the advent of the Portuguese sailing ship opened the great oceans of the West. Whatever the comparison and whatever the causes of the latest shift of power, the fact is that a shift has taken place and larger forces than the existing national ones are being forged to fit the new situation. The strengthening of the European community and the building of a community of free nations in Asia are concomitants of the times and at the same time they are the answer to the Soviet strategy of division and of fear.

Now, in connection with such a policy it is not without point to refer to the debate which has been taking place in this country among thoughtful students, observers and practitioners of American foreign policy. In doing so we come to the fourth major point set forth at the beginning of this chapter and that is the political philosophy which should guide the solutions to our problems of foreign policy.

During the past few years the so-called hardheaded realists have been saying that our policy is muddled by a confusion of morality, sentimentality and idealism. These men demand a cold policy dictated by power and what they term "national self-interest." They claim that many of our difficulties have been caused by deviation from the realistic principles laid down by our early statesmen.

This brief summary does not do justice to the careful thinking which has gone into the various statements of this school of thought. In this book it is not possible to argue the case point by point, or to try to outline the "national self-interest" concept in detail. It is my belief, however, that the "national self-interest" doctrine is neither satisfying nor indeed designed to fill our need for a constructive, consistent policy capable of offsetting the divisive influences at work in the world today.

The United States is directly committed by its history, its form of government, its position in the free world, to the proposition that men are capable of reason, that progress is possible and that our democracy and our policy must be rooted in law and morality.

A policy based on law and morality does not mean a policy of fuzzy sentimentality and unrealizable objectives. Such a policy does not exclude the national self-interest, but it is broader than that. In a world where the masses of people are no longer merely objects of policy, but makers of policy, it is essential that the policy of the United States be based on moral principles. Not long ago the Foreign Minister of Pakistan, in discussing American policy, said: "The world expects more of the United States than it does of Russia or of other countries." Zafrullah Khan's words are true. They show recognition of a real source of our strength among the peoples of the world.

The days are gone by when a Hays, Root or even a Hughes could sit in the old high-ceilinged rooms of the State Department and in good time evolve a policy or treaty to which the people as a whole, except in rare instances, were indifferent. Today every move we make is a matter of immediate concern for our own people and for men and women throughout the world. Today every action we take is an event of hope or fear among the vast populations living near or under the Soviet threat. There are few households in this country which are not touched by our foreign policies. There are few homes without relatives in the armed services in Korea, Germany, Trieste, the British Isles, France or Africa. All of us are acutely affected by the taxes we pay for defense. Our people and the peoples associated with us in the common defense must have faith in what we stand for and in what we are trying to do. Otherwise, they could not and would not carry the burdens now imposed on them.

It is in our national interest to build our policy on foundations of law and morality. They provide the best bastion against the amorality of the Soviets. If we abandoned the moral principles in our policy we would be lost almost before we began in the great struggle with Soviet Communism.

In a free world faced with the divisive forces unleashed by the Soviet Union, in a world whose salvation from all points of view — political, economic and military — is dependent upon a sense of community, what hope would there be of building such a community if the United States could present only a calculated policy of United States national interest to bind nations together? The problem is simply too big to suppose that we can sit in a new Whitehall and delicately balance all these forces with such a doctrine even though we had the most powerful of navies, armies and air forces. Moreover, national interest is not so simple a thing or so clear a guide as it is portrayed to be. As often as not it produces not consistency but inconsistency.

We all look with a certain nostalgia to the days when the world could be dominated by a single navy and the control of a relatively few trade passages and strategic centers. But those days are gone too. We are dealing with an extensive process and with many imponderables and it is only in the broadest sense that we can be ruled by self-interest if we are going to play our part in the preservation of the free world. We must sense the changes that have come about. As the late Professor Collingwood of Oxford wrote: "The chief business of Twentieth-Century philosophy is to reckon with Twentieth-Century history."

On the assumption that the Soviet menace will be with us for some time, it will be necessary for the Western powers to invigorate their community interest. It is also vital that the United States and the great uncommitted areas of the East develop a community interest within the framework of the entire free world.

We have the capacity for coöperative action. We have the capacity for leadership in a partnership. The question is, do we have the means and the wisdom to develop and to execute the policies which will bring us to our goal? That will be examined in the next two chapters.

2

The Making of Policy

The problems outlined in Chapter 1 are packed with political, military, economic and psychological considerations. These considerations play an important part in the making of policy just as each of them places certain limitations on possible solutions and courses of action.

The division of our resources between defense and foreign aid raises a wide gamut of problems relating to our economic and social health, our tax structures, inflation and kindred matters. The division of our resources between ourselves and our friends raises another series of political and economic problems as well as military ones. The economic health and political stability of our associated nations become immediately involved, as does the pace of development of many countries whose condition is asserting a greater and greater pressure on the Western world.

Sound solutions and alternatives require the advice and

judgment of a number of different agencies in different fields. The Department of State and the Department of Defense are always concerned, but so is the Federal Reserve Board, the Treasury and such agencies as are engaged in the administration of our overseas aid or in the control factors of our civilian economy. Many of the problems carry such deep implications they can only be decided by the President. But his decisions in turn can be made effective only with the coöperation of the Congress for it must appropriate the money and pass the laws which make it possible to translate planning into action.

All this demands popular support. Without it Congress cannot be expected to impose the heavy burdens of military service, of taxes, perhaps controls, which are essential to success. With the array of problems world responsibility has put before us, it is more necessary than ever that the individuals and the agencies engaged in the making of foreign policy enjoy the confidence of the people. The basis of our policy must be understood and approved by at least that important section of the population which guides and forms public opinion.

The part which these factors — the political, military, economic, and psychological — play in the making of policy can be illustrated by a problem we have been facing in foreign policy — the problem of a German contribution to European defense.

In 1950, the need for creating an effective defense

for Europe against Soviet aggression became urgent. The question immediately arose of German participation in that defense and the proposal was made that Germany should play her part. Incidentally, it is a mistake to assume that this proposal was exclusively an American one. There was a steady undercurrent of responsible opinion throughout Europe that Germany must be called upon to take part in the defense of Europe.

The Czechoslovak *coup d'etat* of 1948 had laid deep fears of Communist aggression in Europe. But the Communist attack in Korea brought Europe to its feet. The realization that the Soviet was prepared to unleash armed forces to extend its power aroused Europe and particularly Western Germany whose situation presented a parallel unpleasant to contemplate.

First and foremost was the military aspect. Expert military opinion was unanimous that in the event of an attack, an effective defense could not be mustered either against the Soviet or even against those Soviet-satellite military forces which were poised and in reserve west of Russia. This opinion held that two steps had to be taken if a reasonable defense of Europe was to be erected: German participation in defense and a substantial increase of existing western forces. No military opinion, whether French, British, Low Countries or American, took a contrary view. Indeed, this view was pressed by all the Continental staffs. Some political leaders sought a great augmentation of American forces in Europe as a possible substitute for German participation, but for a number of rather obvious reasons, it was realized that this was not a practicable solution.

This unanimous military view was surrounded immediately with political and moral considerations of great moment pro and con a German military contribution. Uppermost was the fear of a revival of German power on the part of Germany's former victims. This was matched by fear on the part of many German leaders of the danger that might arise to their budding democracy through the re-creation of any army. They foresaw that a new German army might seek to play the same role toward Bonn as the Reichswehr had played toward Weimar. Yet paralleling these considerations was the fact that the Western nations would be in an indefensible moral position vis-à-vis the Germans if they denied the Germans any part in their own defense and at the same time showed an unwillingness to assume the responsibility for it themselves.

There were other complexities. The fear, greatly emphasized by the French, that if the Germans had a military force they might drag Europe into a war over the East German territories was opposed by a counter fear; that of the proximity of highly mobilized overpowering Soviet land and air forces which allied forces could not possibly withstand. Unbalanced by counter strength these forces exercised a continuously demoralizing ef-

fect, particularly after the attack on Korea. Finally, the
danger which a separate, armed, nationalistic Germany
might pose was recognized everywhere.

The economic aspects of German rearmament were
also complex. The cost of reconstituting, rearming and
re-equipping German divisions from scratch would en-
tail financial burdens which the new Federal Republic
could not carry alone. Obviously, contributions would
have to be made by the United States, thus again raising
domestic issues in this country. The contribution of the
United States would have to be matched by heavy costs
to the Germans. In turn, this would involve increased
costs to countries such as France and Britain, which
would wish to keep level with German participation. As
a matter of fact, the British argued that they would have
to take their troops out of Germany if they did not
continue to receive so-called Occupation Payments.

Reference has already been made to underlying psychological attitudes in Europe. In France, the indecision
amounting to a political malaise was broken only tem-
porarily by the boldness of the Schuman Plan. After the
first Korean scare many people in Europe and some
prominent political leaders came to the conclusion that
effective defense could only be achieved over a long
period during which the Soviets, provoked by Western
defense measures, might readily overrun Europe. These
Europeans decided, therefore, that it was advantageous

to lie very low, take no action, rely heavily on the strength of the United States, if not its wisdom, and hope for the best.

With this reasoning the neutralist policy flourished everywhere in Europe. In Germany, it was augmented by those who saw the threat of a deeper cleavage with the East Zone if West Germany responded in any way to resist the Communist threat. To offset this thinking, German political leaders had to convey to the people the serious risks of doing nothing, including the danger of a realignment of United States policy.

The limitations which these military, economic, political and psychological factors placed on Western action are painfully apparent. In this situation the divisive talents of the Communists, as one may readily imagine, were given full opportunity for active play. Nevertheless, the Western nations met the complex problems with a bold and constructive answer. They proposed the European Defense Community.

Unfortunately, the EDC has been slow in emerging. Yet, it is a constructive solution which draws the resultant line from a complexity of forces. It deserves our full support. If the European Defense Community does not stand, the effect will be alarming and perhaps disastrous.

The case of German rearmament leading to the European Defense Community is an illustration of a problem on which policy had to be evolved in such a manner as to take into account many limiting factors. It is a problem of policy-making not untypical of the sort which our statesmen must face regularly in the world today.

A complete examination of policy-making would deal with the role of the President, the Congress, the National Security Council, the State Department, the Treasury and Federal Reserve and others. It is beyond the scope of this book to undertake such a survey. One aspect will be covered in this chapter — the relationship between the civilian and military in the making of policy.

Before going into details of this relationship it is important that we should recognize the great contribution our military has made to the protection of this country and of all free nations. Despite the lack of military tradition in the United States and despite the sparse support which the military establishment received from the American people for many years, our military leadership during World War II organized and directed the greatest aggregate of force ever conceived. They did it in a minimum of time. They then proceeded to prosecute a global war successfully both in the East and the West. Yet it will be recalled that this vast military force was allowed by the American people to disintegrate within a matter of only a few months. Then with the Korean crisis, we again called upon our military to defend the free world.

Now it is a cardinal principle of our democratic society that military organizations must be subordinate to civilian authority. In a democracy force must never be the determining factor in reaching solutions. Force must always remain a tool of the democratic state. This principle has been stated and restated during the course of our nation's history. In recent years, however, there has been deep apprehension that the principle has been impaired by the growing influence of military considerations and personalities. It is a concern which has been expressed by both political and military leaders of high standing.

If we are to see the problem in perspective, we must keep in mind that military considerations have over our whole history played a small part in our nation's councils. Henry L. Stimson, former Secretary of State and War, who was always steadfast in upholding the doctrine of civil supremacy, was deeply impressed with the inadequacies and the lack of continuity in our military policy. He believed that this was induced by failure of our political leaders to interest themselves in military affairs. Mr. Stimson frequently said that in the days of the Taft (William Howard) administration when he, Stimson, was Secretary of War for the first time, the tendency of other branches of the government to ignore military or security considerations was both marked and unwise.

Military considerations have been slighted in the determination of our actions despite our rather belligerent national history. For the greater part of our history, military budgets were small affairs. Apart from the attachment that a few senators or congressmen had for naval or military installations in their states, or districts, no interest of consequence could be aroused in military matters.

During the period when there were no apprehensions regarding military influence in our government, many mistakes were made because the recommendations of the professionals were not followed. Shortly after the close of World War I General Pershing, with the assistance of George Marshall, advocated a sound program of manpower utilization and of military policy. Partly because of our then isolationist sentiment but more importantly because of a traditional tendency to disregard military considerations except in time of actual emergency, the adoption of such plans was prevented. Failure to establish a defense program of this type obviously left us without influence when Hitler began to threaten world peace.

From this condition to the enormous development of our military and naval strength in World War II was indeed a mighty step. If military and naval agencies suddenly became unduly powerful, part of the blame must be ascribed to the fact that there was no habit or precedent in the adjustment of military-political considerations during the barren period. Consequently, there was no adequate machinery in existence when war came.

This imbalance in the past certainly does not justify a reversed imbalance in the present. But conditions have greatly changed. The single, most influential domestic factor in the growth of military influence lies in the size of the military budgets. Robert Lovett, former Secretary of Defense, has pointed out the astronomical proportions of the business that he ran. It dwarfs the accumulation of most of the big industries of the country. There is scarcely a congressional district that does not now have a military installation or one sufficiently close by to be influenced by it. Congressmen, generally, are keenly interested in these installations. Moreover, they are deeply concerned with the manpower policies of the Defense Departments. These factors have had a most powerful effect in the growth of military influence in our government.

The deep political and economic implications of our assumption of world leadership and of the growth of our military power unfortunately did not lead to a corresponding increase in the influence, prestige or capacity of the civilian agencies of our government. Indeed, with the attack on Pearl Harbor, there was almost a complete abandonment by the political agencies of any further direction of foreign affairs except in the noncombatant areas. This may have been influenced to a degree by a conflict of personalities in the State Department. But there was a deeper reason. The isolationism of the 1920–1940 period had produced a vacuum of political objectives. The State Department did not have, indeed it was not encouraged to have, any political aims in the world. More thinking along political lines was being done and being asserted in the Munitions Building — this was before the era of the Pentagon — than in the old State Building.

It was due in large part to the experience and inclinations of Secretary Stimson that this political-military thinking was encouraged in the War Department. It was due to his initiative that regular meetings between the Secretary of State, the Secretary of the Navy, and the Secretary of War were set up to deal with such questions. The meetings were helpful, but as there was no secretariat to regularize procedures and no authority to carry through judgments to action, they were only spasmodically effective. However, out of this came SWNC, and out of SWNC came the National Security Council.

Another factor of considerable importance during the war helped materially to increase the power and the prestige of the military. It lay in the personality of the President and his strong disposition to deal as Commander-in-Chief with the uniformed officers of the Armed Forces to the exclusion not only of the Secretary of State, but also of the Secretaries of War and Navy. In matters relating to the Navy, the President felt little need for intermediate civilian advice. Although President Roosevelt had a very high respect for Mr. Stimson, it was his habit to consult him relatively infrequently and only on the broadest Army and Air Force questions. The President preferred to go directly to General Marshall and to General Arnold or through Mr. Hopkins or Admiral Leahy to these officers or others on matters related to military operations. This led to a disposition to get on with winning the war as quickly as possible to the exclusion of political objectives. And, no doubt, it did result in a prompter military victory.

The President's consultations with his uniformed officers — unlike those of his distinguished colleague in victory, Mr. Churchill — rarely resulted in the imposition of his views on the military but rather in his acceptance, almost without question, of the views of the military. In this connection General Marshall was assiduous and conscientious in informing Mr. Stimson of all his contacts with the White House. Indeed, General Marshall did all in his power to stimulate greater contact between the President and the Secretary's office.

A factor of great importance in the influence of the military in the United States is the habit of direct contact of the uniformed officers with the Congress. Unlike the British ministerial system which provides the method of dealing with Parliament, there has always been direct contact in this country between the military and Congress. Long before the war the ability of officers to make this contact and cement their relations with the Legislature had tended to dilute the influence of the civilian members of the defense agencies in their congressional relations.

Contacts are made, hearings are scheduled as a matter

of routine with little or no intervention on the part of civilians. This is not the result of a sinister conspiracy by any means and there have been few instances where the relationship has been abused. It is because the defense departments are so organized that there are simply not enough civilians sufficiently well informed and experienced to be able to handle all the necessary relationships between the defense agencies and the Congress. During the war, even with the great influx into Washington of civilians in the production and procurement field, the Congress tended to place its greatest reliance upon the uniformed officers. Moreover, Congressmen insisted on dealing directly with the officers. Under these circumstances, the better-prepared men of the uniformed forces quite naturally asserted the larger influence.

In the field of foreign policy, the influence of the military has also become very heavy. This is a natural development in a world where power is a prime determinant. Until forty years ago the United States was far from the center of the great struggles of the world. Now we are in the midst of them. Our power makes us the leading member of the community of nations opposed to the Communist threat. The various members look to us for military leadership and coördination. Our officers are chosen as Supreme Commanders for NATO and for the forces of the United Nations. Our commitments have placed us in a position of immediate involvement in extensive areas of the world. It is obvious, therefore, that military interests will play a large part in the considerations dictating our policy.

The habit of confining large questions on the conduct of the war to purely military considerations, which President Roosevelt instituted and which was almost unconsciously carried on by his successor, was strikingly exemplified by a conference which took place in the White House in June, 1945.

After the surrender of the German forces, but before Potsdam and before the Japanese surrender, President Truman, at the instigation of the Joint Chiefs of Staff, called a meeting to consider the type of operations our future campaign against Japan should take. The particular question posed was whether an attack should be launched on the main islands of Japan, and if so, which ones. But the general question presented related to the whole course of future operations necessary to bring about a Japanese surrender.

The Joint Chiefs were present. The Secretary of War was present for at least a part of the time and one of his representatives. Neither the Secretary of State nor any of his representatives attended.

After putting the question to the President, the Joint Chiefs proposed an early attack on Kyushu, presenting an estimate of the time necessary to mount the attack, the likely casualties, and the probable results. It was suggested that this attack should be followed up by a much heavier one on Honshu and across the Tokyo plain. Together the plans amounted to a major operation.

The prospect of an attack on the main Japanese islands, even at that late date, was not too attractive. Memories of the beaches and uplands of Tarawa, Iwo Jima and Okinawa were in everyone's minds, yet no alternative to this course was proposed. The Chiefs of Staff of the respective services were unanimous as to the necessity of the operation.

The President, conscious of his heavy responsibility, individually polled all the Chiefs present and then rendered his decision: attack Kyushu; plan for Honshu, but return for further instructions before the preparations arrived at a point beyond which there would not be further opportunity for a free choice on the part of the President.

It is necessary for a full understanding of this incident to recall for a moment the background of the conference. The greatest enemy military force in Europe had recently surrendered without condition. Great Britain and the United States possessed between them what was incomparably the greatest naval force the world had ever seen. We possessed an air superiority over Japan so overwhelming as to be almost fantastic.

We had an impregnable moral position before Japan and the world. We had advanced across the Pacific to the main islands after an act of outrageous aggression on the part of Japan. On top of it all, we possessed the secret of the atom bomb. All present in the room knew that the scientists and engineers working on that project had given definite assurances that within a very short period of time an atomic explosion embodying military consequences of great significance would occur. Other points of superiority could be recounted.

After the President's decision had been made and the conference was breaking up, an official, not theretofore participating, suggested that serious attention should be given to a political attempt to end the war. The meeting fell into a tailspin, but after control was recovered, the idea appealed to several present. It appealed particularly to the President, and to one member of the Joint Chiefs of Staff, who, by the way, was the one member of that body who had no responsibility to a particular service.

It was also at this meeting that the suggestion was first broached that warning be given the Japanese of our possession of the bomb before we dropped it. Although all present were "cleared," the uninhibited mention of the "best-kept secret of the war" caused a sense of shock, even among that select group.

Now this incident indicates that at that time everyone was so intent on winning the war by military means that the introduction of political considerations was almost accidental. It cannot be charged against the military that they did not initially put forward the suggestion of political action. It was not their job to do so. Nor did any one of them oppose the thought of political action, though several of the Chiefs were not too happy about it. Not one of the Chiefs nor the Secretary thought well of a bomb warning, an effective argument being that no one could be certain, in spite of the assurances of the scientists, that the "thing would go off." At that time, we had not yet had the benefit of the Alamogordo test.

As a result of the meeting, a rather hastily composed paper was drawn up. It embodied the idea which later formed the basis of the appeal to the Japanese to surrender. That proposal, it will be recalled, was refused brusquely by the Japanese Government. Yet, as we now know, it did provoke considerable discussion and divergence of opinion among the Japanese military leaders and politicians. It is interesting to speculate whether, better prepared, this proposal might not have included statements of the policy which we put into effect in Japan almost immediately after the war ended. Such a proposal might well have induced surrender without the use of the bomb. What effect that might have had on postwar developments is a subject worthy of conjecture.

Although no one from the State Department was present at the conference which has been described, Mr. Joseph Grew for some time had been most energetically urging a political approach to the Japanese, but his thoughts never seemed effectively to have gotten to the White House, at least prior to the June meeting.

Though we have a tendency to blame the decisions that were taken at Yalta and Potsdam for many of the postwar difficulties with the Soviet Union, events were forming a pattern for our postwar fate before those conferences ever took place. We concentrated so heavily on the actual conduct of the war that we overlooked the need for political thinking. We acted as if we were utterly unaware of the fully advertised objectives of the Communists and of earlier disclosures of their methods of operation. The pressing danger of a Nazi victory, of course, helped to blind us. But certainly too little emphasis was placed on such collateral political considerations as the likely course of postwar Soviet policy. In condemning the government, however, we must recall that few people outside the government took a different view. There was little or no hard-headed analysis of Soviet intentions on the part of intellectuals or any other public opinion leaders of the time. As a matter of fact, the tendency was to be sentimental about them.

The events and considerations described here in connection with the ending of the war with Japan and with the more recent problem of German rearmament make this conclusion evident: our military leaders must have the widest appreciation of the limiting and tempering influence of political and economic considerations upon courses of action which strictly military considerations would dictate. This does not mean that it is the job of the military to work out political solutions. It does mean that the military must have a deeper understanding of the relationship of political and economic problems to military matters. They must be prepared to coöperate in working out combined solutions in which military aspects may have to be modified or even sacrificed in order to give the necessary weight to considerations of a political, economic or psychological nature.

Our military people have made large strides in recent years in broadening their understanding of the non-military factors involved in policy. Perhaps one of the reasons may be institutional. The breadth of thinking in political matters at the National War College, administered directly by the Joint Chiefs of Staff, is impressive. It is interesting that there is no similar civilian or State Department school to which the future generals may repair to receive training in political and economic studies. The Foreign Service Institute as presently constituted does not remotely resemble the National War College. Such an institution, if it existed, might help the military become as aware of political interests as the State Department officials are of military considerations.

Although it has been suggested that the name of the War College be changed and that it be conducted as a full joint operation of the Departments of State and Defense, there is reason to doubt whether this is the full solution. State Department officers require a greater sophistication in political matters than the War College now gives. Although the future generals are rather well equipped politically by these courses for their military duties, this instruction does not go far enough for the future political leaders. Military officers should certainly not be excluded from this fuller political sophistication, nor should a political college, such as suggested here, fail to deal seriously with military matters. There are some who feel that such a course would be better conducted in our universities or in a number of institutions connected with universities throughout the country. The advantage which the government institution has is that it is closer to the center of responsibility and to the realities of policy-making.

Since this is a general discussion of the military and civilian roles in the making of policy, a few words about the Joint Chiefs of Staff are in order. They play an important part in policy-making. Any development which would help them merge individual service points of view into a broader approach would aid in the formation of national policy. Many improvements have been made in the matter of politico-military relationships since the war. Easy and profitable contact is now going on between the State and Defense Departments. Yet I have the impression that today the Joint Chiefs of Staff have become much more of a bottleneck in the desirable flow of decisions which finally constitute our policy than they were in World War II days when their status was less formalized than it is now. Papers and discussion have deteriorated somewhat in quality.

A number of reasons are given for this deterioration. It is said that there is a tendency on the part of the military to claim a military interest in decisions where military interest is relatively remote. It is alleged that the quality of the professional staff is not as high as it used to be. Another reason ascribed has already been suggested — that the respective members of the Joint Chiefs of Staff show too close an attachment to their particular service.

I feel that many difficulties and impasses which arose in connection with the work of the Joint Chiefs of Staff in wartime were attributable to attachment to service interest on the part of certain members of the Joint Chiefs of Staff. My inclination would be therefore to study carefully, without accepting in its entirety, the suggestion of Dr. Vannevar Bush, whose experience is more recent than mine, for the divorcement of the Joint Chiefs of Staff from the services. I do not believe that it is possible organizationally to separate policy entirely from operations. The Joint Chiefs must have significant authority and command as a group or else their influence would quickly dwindle to the level of the old Naval Board of Strategy. But they should be relieved of the responsibility for the administration of the services. They should be put in a position to develop over-all judgments, give directives for joint missions and not be limited by the viewpoint of the individual services.

Dr. Bush has also made the suggestion, which should be supported, that the Joint Chiefs of Staff should as a normal procedure channel their recommendations through the Secretary of Defense. They should not, according to him, have direct access to the President or the National Security Council, save through a certain right of appeal if they feel that their views are being dangerously disregarded. Even with such an experienced man as President Roosevelt at the helm, the exclusive President-Joint Chiefs of Staff relationship was not the best method of conducting a war, despite the fact that it was won hands down. The influence of the civilian Secretary of Defense should be increased by interposing him or his representative as a matter of custom between the military and the President. This is a long way from suggesting that the civilian secretaries should interpose themselves in military operations. We want no repetition of the Battle of Bladensburg where, according to the legend, a Secretary of War took the field and shortly thereafter Washington was taken and the White House burned.

Uniformed officers should have wide contacts and a constant interchange of ideas with the civilian heads of the Defense Departments. There is, or at least there used to be, a definite and sometimes studied tendency in some quarters for the professionals to go about their business unafflicted by civilian influence. Secretary Forrestal used to refer to the analogy of an ant riding a log on its way down the Mississippi River and feeling very puffed up about it. Civilians in the Defense Departments, including himself, he used to say, sometimes thought they were directing a very large operation, but all they were doing, unless they made themselves quite obnoxious, was to go along for the ride.

From the foregoing the conclusion emerges that serious consideration should be given to:

a. making the Joint Chiefs of Staff more independent of their respective services while retaining with their command authority over operations;

b. having the Joint Chiefs of Staff normally report through the Defense Secretary to the President;

c. re-surveying the relationship between uniformed officers and the Congress.

While our military men should be sensitive to political factors, they should exercise greater restraint in expressing views in public on political subjects. Failure to do this injures their own profession; puts the cat among the pigeons abroad where pronouncements on political matters by the military have too many historical connotations; and tends to weaken a fundamental principle of a democracy that on political matters the civilians' should be the dominant voice.

Although the influence of the military should not be dominant, their thinking should not be suppressed. What is needed is a sharp increase in the vigor and prestige of the civilian authority and particularly of the State Department. It is obvious that development in the power and quality of the State Department has not kept pace with our needs.

If the State Department is to dominate the making

of our policy, there must be the quality of thought and vigor of action which justify domination. After all, we are not seeking civilian domination per se, we are seeking a sound, courageous and imaginative policy.

Perhaps it was too much to expect that the Department could keep pace with the increase of military influence in time of war, but the extensive abandonment of authority in the political field which followed Pearl Harbor was a large step toward the lowered influence of the State Department. Moreover, that great persuader, the purse, was not in the hands of the State Department officials as it has been in the hands of the military.

To be sure, the State Department had men who were engaged in peace-planning. Owing, however, to President Roosevelt's preoccupation in winning the war as rapidly as possible by military means and because of his contacts with the military to the exclusion of the political agencies, these planners were not meshed into policy. Then there was the fact that the active, energetic new blood which was infused into the Washington scene during the war period largely went into the War Department, Lend Lease, the Armed Forces — everywhere, it seems, except the State Department. Going into the State Department in time of war did not have the same appeal as going into the Armed Services or the Defense Departments.

So much for background. Now what can we do to raise civilian influence and particularly the State Department to the level of its duties and responsibilities?

In the first place, we must have at home the machinery for maintaining a proper balance of the political, military and economic interests. The National Security Council was established to do this, but it is not yet in a position to meet the full need. Above all, we must have officials in the State Department who have political vision and the ability to foresee and act upon vital world problems. They must have the capacity to develop long-range programs for our security and that of the free world. Though they must have a full realization of the limitations which military and economic considerations impose, they must have courage, initiative and force in the political field. There must be a greater sense of the urgency of anticipating problems. They must be prepared to put forward creative proposals and they must not fold up at the first negative paper which emanates from the Pentagon, however formidably it is presented.

Now these are generalities but they have great implications in terms of the tradition and personnel of the State Department. They involve a shedding of the stultifying process of too much cable sending and answering. So much emphasis is put on the day-to-day cables and on reporting that little time is left for planning.

The routine of Foreign Service work as it is now carried on does not attract the more active and energetic types of minds. Anticipation of trouble and finding constructive means to avoid it are activities which are not sufficiently developed or applauded. Many thorny but observable problems have been heading toward us for a long time but the tendency has been to put off dealing with them, partly because of the succession of current headaches but also just because they are troublesome. For example, such matters as the Saar and the Kuriles ought to have been dealt with earlier when each of them was much easier of solution. There are others of similar character and the attack on the long range problems such as the development of Asia and Africa ought not to be further postponed.

Some form of institutional training should be devised to stimulate the qualities needed by our Foreign Service officers. We can learn from the experience of other services. The school system of the military and naval forces is well worth considering. Graduating from a basic institution such as one of the Academies, the young officer is imbued with a sense of dedication to his country and to his work at the same time he is receiving his technical training. But this is only the beginning of his education. Every few years, at least, the most promising military officers are sent back to school, sometimes to a service school, frequently to a university. The best of them go on to Command and General Staff schools and finally to the National War College. They have the consciousness that they are being trained for high positions and responsibility. They are not sent to school because they can be spared, but because they give promise of decisive thought and action. The State Department might well copy this pattern. The emergence alone of the Far East, Middle East, Near East and Africa into the forefront of our policy would justify more intensive and continued study through such an institution.

There is another important deficiency in the organization of the work of the State Department. Not enough responsibility is delegated to the men in the field. This is not a situation that can be easily overcome. Congress has been reluctant to permit the State Department to exercise wide authority. Consequently, the State Department cannot delegate to its officers authority which it does not itself fully possess. The military have this authority. Once a course of action has been determined, the military gives its theater and area commanders definite authority to carry out the policy.

Despite these difficulties, there is need and there is room for greater decentralization of authority in the State Department. Without it young men are not encouraged to develop the assurance and initiative necessary to fill important policy-making posts. Thus they are prone to yield a political position to strongly stated military considerations backed by all the prestige and incidental influence which the uniform can muster.

There have been men in the State Department who have had invaluable experience in the exercise of authority. They received it largely in connection with overseas occupation work where, by necessity, the lines of authority back to Washington have been less tight than is usually the case. Many of these men have not been Foreign Service officers in the technical sense and they have frequently found difficulty in obtaining positions within the Department. This illustrates the fact that, without a more competitive system of training and experience than exists at present and without the establishment of career planning and management, too much emphasis is placed upon personal relationships.

In view of the extensive requirements which our role of world leadership places upon us for knowledgeable public servants, there is need for a sort of "Royal Commission" to give high level consideration to the following:

(1) the requirements of government and private industry for men and women with broad backgrounds in foreign affairs;

(2) the establishment of a new governmental school of foreign affairs for civilians in government which would develop men and women capable of insuring civilian domination in the conduct of our foreign relations.

There is always danger of over-simplification or exaggeration in comments on the State Department. The problem of increased civilian influence must not be treated as a matter which can be brought about simply by issuing an order or passing a law. Some devices can be properly employed to restore a proper balance. Primarily, the need is constantly to stimulate, train and test Foreign Service officers to the point where they can stand up for their political judgments against pressures with a confidence born of their own active competence and responsibility. With such competence and confidence the civilian authority can overcome barriers and effectively reassert its role of leadership in foreign affairs. Here it must be added that the unquestioned loyalty, integrity and devotion to duty of the overwhelming number of State Department officials merit the confidence of the American public.

The making of far-sighted foreign policy depends upon the capacity of individuals to weigh the relationship of many components, particularly those of a political, economic, military, and psychological character. There must be close coöperation among men who are not only well trained in their own fields, but who are also capable of sensing and weighing the limitations imposed by other factors.

Close coördination within our own government, however, is not enough. A similar capacity for working out joint solutions with the representatives of other nations is essential.

Military agencies have kept pace with the developments brought about by two world wars and their influence and prestige have greatly increased, while the influence and prestige of the State Department have not. The thinking of military officers should not be suppressed, but it should be broadened to include more than purely military factors. The military should be made more sensitive of the limitations that political and economic forces must play. It has been suggested that certain devices might be considered in order to augment civilian influence in the making of policy but fundamentally the problem is not one of procedure but of substance.

Our primary objective is to find the ways and means to create sound and constructive policy, policy which will be best designed to protect our security and that of the free world. It is essential that the civilian agencies should be stimulated to think along these lines. Only in this way will the quality of civilian thinking merit the influence it can and should assert in a democratic society.

The training and responsibility of Foreign Service officers should be strengthened and their contacts with intellectual, scientific and commercial activities in the nation should be increased. There should be renewed effort to recruit top-flight students from the colleges and graduate schools on the basis of the complex and fascinating challenges that our present position in the world presents.

An improvement in the processes by which policy is made is only the beginning and not the end of the task. Policy can be made effective only by an extensive process carried out in the field. The execution of policy in the field places many demands on our representation abroad. In the next chapter an attempt will be made to cover the new techniques and approaches needed in carrying out our policy.

3

The Execution of Policy

We must now try to deal with some of the complexities involved in the execution of policy. In doing so, emphasis will be placed upon the American representative abroad.

We have pointed out earlier that the major aim of American policy must be to bring the free nations together in community projects so that these nations will be in a position (1) to advance their own freedom and prosperity and (2) to prevent the further divisive influence of Soviet Communism. Such a policy means that the American representative abroad has two major and inseparable tasks: he must interpret the United States, its aims, its aspirations, its culture, to the country in which he is stationed; equally important, he must help to identify the common interests and ideas that bind nations together, and aid in overcoming old suspicions, jealousies and other disruptive tendencies.

The role of mediator and helper is not an easy one

among individuals; it is a more difficult one among nations. The difficulty is compounded by the anti-American feeling which is prevalent in Europe — and perhaps elsewhere in the world — and by the passionate efforts of the Communists to stir it up. In their effort to block the growth of the European community the Communists put heavy emphasis on the stimulation of these anti-American attitudes. They recognize that American policy and influence tend to bring free peoples and nations together. They know that if they can damage our influence they will be successful in destroying the European community projects.

The importance which the Kremlin places on the divisive role of the Soviet Union could not be more clearly evidenced than it was in Stalin's October manifesto. Communist doubters were beginning to question the doctrine of the inevitability of dissension and inter-destruction of the free nations, particularly in the light of the growing Soviet menace to those nations. The late Soviet dictator put them in their place with a denunciation which reveals (a) the Kremlin's real concern over unity of action among the free peoples and (b) the Kremlin's determination to prevent this unity by pursuing vigorously the old Communist line of dissension and division, particularly by developing hostility toward the United States.

Even were we not faced with this anti-American sentiment abroad, the point that our foreign representation requires new techniques would in my judgment be valid. Our representatives — if they are to be successful — should be fully sensitive, though not over-sensitive, to this atmosphere of irritation if not of hostility toward the United States. They must be sensitive to all its aspects — historical, political, economic and cultural — even though in many instances the expression of this feeling is provincial rather than rational.

Now, this atmosphere does not reflect a simple or precise emotion. Among the peoples of Europe and elsewhere there is, of course, a wide, fundamental feeling of friendship for the United States. There is substantial recognition of the role we have played in assuaging human misery and in reëstablishing their economies, and of our attachment to the concepts of liberty and individual rights.

Europeans do not fear territorial encroachments or exploitation by the United States. Yet even among those who are fundamentally well disposed toward the American colossus there is an indisputable degree of jealousy and of irritation toward us. Among the political leaders and the intellectuals there is a widespread disposition to question our ability to carry out a steady policy. Among the leaders there is, if not an anti-American feeling, at least what one might call a skepto-American feeling.

Europeans look back to the days of their own power and resent its transfer to the United States. They feel the need of compensation and they fill it to a large extent with criticism of our culture and our manners. All aspects of modern civilization which the European intellectual decries are apt to be labeled "American." We are sometimes made responsible for economic and social ills that were not unknown in ancient Greece and Rome. Moreover, it is important to recognize that Karl Marx is involved in the process and that his influence extends far beyond Communist ranks. Today, by the use of some clever propaganda, Marx's *Das Kapital* and the entire Marxian analysis, which were based on a study of conditions in England, France and Germany many generations ago, are made to appear as if they had been inspired by present-day American "exploitation and capitalism."

This thinking has cut deep into areas where one would imagine that America would find evident understanding. The European Socialists come particularly to mind. Their attitude deserves some consideration.

In Germany, in the United Kingdom, in France and elsewhere in Europe, the Socialists have developed a certain coolness toward the United States. This is disturbing because the Socialist movement is old and established in Europe and large segments among the Socialists are liberal-minded individuals. In spite of their utter failure to exert influence on each other in the avoidance of European wars, the Socialists generally represent a democratic force. They are almost uniformly bitterly opposed to Soviet Communism. This cannot be said of their extreme left-wingers but it can be of the general mass of these parties. Nevertheless, the Socialist attitude, though not violently hostile, is one of skepticism bordering on ideological antagonism to the United States.

The Socialist economic ideology tends to class the American economic system into Marx's concept of ruthless capitalism and exploitation of the masses. Some objective-minded German Socialists tried with some success to dispel this concept in Germany after visiting this country and seeing our system in action. Unfortunately, they have not fully eliminated the misconceptions of their party associates.

The advantages of the American system and its departures from the backward capitalism which has in the past characterized European life are largely unknown among the rank and file of the Socialists of Europe. Moreover, the very fact that the American economy has been successful in distributing its advantages in a classless manner stirs some of the doctrinaire Socialists into a sort of ideological antagonism that cannot be ignored.

The essential element is that these anti-American emotions constitute a political fact. And the Communists are making the most of it — witness the Communist Manifesto in Germany late in 1952 in which all party members were urged to ally themselves firmly with the Socialists though not with their leaders. Anti-Americanism is a technique used by the Communists to achieve long-standing goals. The Communists are not merely fighting to defeat American aims in Europe, they are seeking to remake European society in their image. An American labor leader, whose task it is to work with the free unions in Europe, has said that we should not talk of Communist penetration in France and Italy but rather of the Communist "investment" in Europe.

Ever since World War I Communist leaders and cells have been at work in France and Italy, in Germany and elsewhere, planting and nurturing their seeds. They have tried to bring up a generation of pro-Communist European intellectuals, workers and farmers; they have sought to condition the people of Europe to respond to problems with Communist ideas and prejudices. No consideration of the future of Europe, of the stand such countries as France, Italy and others might take in a crisis, can afford to lose sight of this situation. This is one of the basic problems facing American representation abroad and it is one which must be dealt with. The key to coöperation with these groups must be found for they constitute, in the main, real bulwarks of representative government.

Such is the situation in which an American representative abroad finds himself. It is a situation in which there is apt to be hostility to the purposes of his mission and jealousy of the power he represents. It is apparent that to be successful in his mission of interpreting the United States abroad and developing unity among the free nations, the American representative must possess the vision of the statesman, the insight of the philosopher and the healing powers of the doctor.

The job of the American representative in Europe — and elsewhere in the world — is no longer that of the King's messenger, transmitting notes, cabling back replies and sending interminable reports on the situation. His task is to participate and coöperate in the development of all policies that bring free peoples and nations together.

The American representative abroad should not attempt to build backfires against governments in power, and must not interfere with local interests and be in favor of or against parties or personalities. But there is a wide area where there are legitimate interests in connection with building the community. In that respect, we are interested, for example, in the budget of France, in the economic stability of the country, in the flow of its tax revenues, in the leadership of its trade unions. For their part the French have a right to be interested in the status and availability of our manpower, in the division of our resources, in the quantity and quality of our aid. They have a right to know that we will not permit the development of another totalitarian menace in Germany. They have a right to be attentive to our situation, and we have a right to be attentive to their condition. That is the meaning of community of interest.

The task of representation demands different approaches. In Germany, it is the task of American representation to demonstrate the need for the European community, the opportunities in it, the danger if it is not realized. The American representative is in a position to demonstrate that we seek no material advantages from the Germans; that our presence guarantees that there will be no discrimination against Germany within the common alliance; above all, that we are prepared to support the new Germany in its efforts to strengthen its democratic regime and democratic institutions within the European community.

In France there are different demands on our representation. The United States understands the fears which still persist in France of Germans in uniform. This country has sympathy for French reluctance to contemplate the re-emergence of German industrial and political power. It is the job of our representation in France to convince the French that we will not permit the domination of France by Germany; that the best way to avoid it is to blend Germany into the European community. It is also necessary to remind France that she should have the courage of her own proposals and traditions and that she cannot continue to vacillate between two fears.

In Britain the task is staked out by the same over-all political goal of community. Her position presents difficulties but her economy and her defense demand the closest association with those who share her interests. It is the job of our representation to help convince the

British that they should support the European community and stand in close contact with it. It is the job of our representation to demonstrate to all sections of the British people that we are seeking to gain peace and freedom through a pooling of our common strength.

The American job in NATO bears similar characteristics. General Eisenhower's great achievement at SHAPE was the establishment of a team, devising common plans and setting up a common force to meet the common danger. His was the job of a moderator as well as leader; his was a job of inspiration.

In all countries it is important to interpret the economic position of the United States to governments and peoples. It is necessary for them to understand that there is a limit to our available resources and that an economic collapse in the United States would be in sight if we continued to spend at an unrestricted rate. There is a limit to our bounty if we are to play a continuously constructive role as a coöperating partner of all free peoples.

It is obvious that to meet these tasks American representation in the field must be vigorous, self-reliant, well-informed, active. Above all, American representatives must have a large degree of independence. I do not mean that American ambassadors should be in a position to form their own independent foreign policies. I mean they must have freedom of action in implementing the over-all policy of unity. They must not be confined to reading stacks of cables all signed by the Secretary of

State who could not possibly have written or seen one one-hundredth of them. They should not be tied down to either end of the teletype machine or mailbox.

The American representative must be free to get around and travel without reporting from every whistle-stop to the home station. In implementing a community policy it is no longer possible for a representative to maintain relations with one Foreign Office only. Views must be exchanged in various capitals. During the months in which the Schuman Plan and European Defense arrangements were discussed and negotiated, it was necessary certainly for the American representative in Germany to spend a large amount of time in Paris, London, Brussels and elsewhere. This close but informal contact with the other representatives of the region can be of great value. In connection with such developments as the European community the importance of regional representation has emerged. As this develops, a radical revision of traditional forms will ensue but that should not deter the Department from necessary action.

To achieve his task the American representative needs a large grant of authority as well as of independence. There should be no doubt in the minds of the foreign political leaders with whom he talks that, within the area staked out by the over-all policy of his government, he is in a position to exercise his own imagination and ideas and that his words and actions are fully supported at home. In order to give our foreign representatives the opportunity to operate as the final authority abroad, the disposition of our economic and military aid programs, subject to over-all policy laid down by Washington, should repose in each country in the head of the United States Mission. If somewhere else in the Ambassador's jurisdiction there is another American agency which can dispose of funds, it will only be a short time before the influence of the chief United States authority in the land is seriously diluted. In some areas the dilution of the authority of the Chief of Mission has reached fantastic proportions. If our purpose is to build up the initiative, capacity and influence of our foreign representatives, they should be able to look forward to supreme authority in the field. This authority was united in the chief of the United States mission in Germany and it worked well.

It is no answer to say that the Congress does not repose sufficient faith in the State Department representatives to grant this authority to them, for one of the quickest ways to impair the integrity and capacity of our State Department officials abroad is to dilute their authority by setting up three or four coördinate agencies beside them. In some quarters there is a certain nostalgic yearning for the old days of dignified and stately diplomatic exchanges, unhampered by economic and informational activities. Those days are gone, as Jim Fisk used to say, "where the woodbine twineth." I personally think it is a mistake to separate these modern weapons of diplomacy from the State Department. If they are to be separated, however, they should be controlled and directed, in the field, by the Chief of Mission, and everybody should know that they are subject to his authority.

There is another aspect of representation which is of fundamental significance. The statesmen and people of Europe and the world must have faith in the integrity of American policy and American representation. Other nations may have had a degree of success in playing off one power against the other. America's role today is quite different. It is a uniting process and in such a process it is of vital importance that we be forthright and say and mean the same to each.

There is another level at which the emphasis on divisive tactics on the part of the Communists demands representation. That is at the level of the people themselves. It is the task and the great need today of the American representative to interpret the United States, its policies, its aims and its methods to broad sections of the people of the country to which he is accredited. The state of opinion in many countries demands a portrayal of the United States as it is and not as it is being distorted. To be effective, this approach must be frank and aboveboard. Such representation will do more than any covert contacts possibly can.

Representation of this type calls for a constant exchange of views with all elements of the population. It was my experience that an evening of discussion with farmer or labor groups in Germany, with the editors and publishers, with university men and women, with heads of women's or youth organizations was far more useful and interesting than attendance at any diplomatic reception.

It is not easy to do all this. It is infinitely more profitable, though more fatiguing, to hold these informal meetings with students and professors, writers and scientists, social workers and businessmen, than it is to make the rounds of all the social functions in a capital. This is all rather obvious but a meeting which took place at my home in Berlin during the great Communist Youth Rally of August, 1951, is a good illustration of the usefulness of such meetings.

For that giant propaganda effort hundreds of thousands, indeed, about a million, East Zone German youth had been marshaled into East Berlin to demonstrate against the West, particularly against the United States. These young people, representing the youth of East Germany, were gathered together by the Communists in an effort to achieve a great political advantage. Yet they were young human beings and like most others, inquisitive and vigorous. They were not satisfied with the tribunes and regimented displays in the East Sector of Berlin and vast numbers of them swarmed into the Western Sectors. They quickly felt and saw the differences between the freedoms of the West and the labored demonstrations and oppressions of the East.

We managed to pick up a score of these young people from the streets and have them in for lunch. They were badly dressed, sallow, hungry. Although it was obvious they had not been converted by the Communists, it was equally clear that Communist propaganda had made them suspicious of the United States. Over a New England boiled luncheon these young people asked intelligent, incisive questions about the United States, our aims, our economy, our plans for Germany. They came for lunch, but they remained until dinner. When they left they had some new perspectives and so did we. Later, after they had returned into the anonymity of the East Zone, we received evidence that this contact and many similar contacts which East Zone youths had been able to make in West Berlin during the rally, had had a profound effect throughout all East Germany. Parenthetically it is interesting to note that the Communist leaders staged the next rally in Leipzig where there are no West Sectors.

The American representative is in a position to demonstrate that the American people carry extremely heavy burdens and are making large sacrifices in an effort to build a community of interest with the peoples of the world. He can show that we have a common purpose above mere defense. And he can give proof that their worries are basically not different from or heavier than those of other peoples with whom they must now coöperate. Of course there must go with this interpretation a determined attempt to understand the aspirations, the culture, the "ethos" of the people of the country to which he is accredited. This likewise takes time and effort, but it is more frequently attempted and successfully achieved than the more difficult and frequently less attractive task of interpreting to other people the true spirit of the people of the United States.

The United States has seen examples of foreign representatives within this country who have carried out their mission in this spirit. During the war Lord Halifax, the British Ambassador, spared himself no fatigue and no indignity in interpreting the British Isles and the actions and aspirations of the British people to the people of the United States. More recently, his successors, Lord Inverchapel and Sir Oliver Franks, carried on in the same spirit. From the reports it would appear that Mr. Bowles in India did the same sort of thing as our representative in that critical area of the world, and Mrs. Anderson in Denmark has been another example.

Sir Richard Casey, the Foreign Minister of Australia, recently said that here and there in every country there were men and women who have the ability to communicate and some who, as he put it, were "touched by the Hand of God," with insight to understand and influence peoples. He said that a serious effort should be made to identify these men and women and make it possible for them to exert their genius in stimulating other people to develop their latent powers. Sir Richard probably had in mind some of the remarkable men who were developed by the British out of their wide contacts and understanding with native races. Not many of us enjoy this state of Grace nor should I suggest that our representatives abroad be turned into diplomatic St. Pauls. But there is an element in modern representation abroad which is quite new, very important and demanding of new techniques. Official contacts are primary and will continue to be so. But the limitations which surround official negotiations can be made less restrictive through emphasis upon this phase of representation.

We are dealing with movements today rather than with national problems. It is not possible to cope with such movements effectively by delivering *aide-memoires* to the Foreign Office. There must even be a sacrifice of the time presently devoted to kind, friendly, but numerically taxing, fellow countrymen who, for a strange reason, include the American Ambassador and his staff among the "musts" on a sightseeing tour.

The kind of United States representation abroad which has been described here goes beyond traditional diplomatic practice. It has been the custom apart from a relatively few dignified appearances at properly arranged functions to deal only with governments and to look upon activities beyond this as imprudent or as intervention in the domestic affairs of other sovereign states. It is questionable whether this meets the modern need.

The Soviet Union attempts and in large measure succeeds in carrying its aggression to every village and every level of society. Our problem is to provide helpful leadership of free peoples in such a way that the distinction between leadership and aggression is clearly understood. If we succeed in doing this, the Communist psychological trick of accusing the United States of doing what the Soviet itself does, and even worse, would carry no conviction.

American representation abroad which devotes itself to an understanding of respected partners with whom we seek to identify and cultivate common aspirations will make a large contribution in overcoming misunderstanding and in clarifying the distinction between aggression and leadership. Such representation approaches its task with humility. It evolves its thinking through consultation instead of imposition.

In implementing our foreign policy, we have just begun to scratch the surface in formulating with other free peoples the objectives which we share together. For instance, we have hardly begun to understand the seriousness of Soviet ideology as a threat to the religious foundations of our free societies. The religious faiths of the non-Communist world could constitute a cohesive moral force which could combat successfully the artificial materialism of Communism. The common yearning for protection from war and from mass destruction needs further exploration and definition. Likewise, the freedom of each nation to evolve its own way of life without interference from any outside nation needs further exploration with our friends. These are some of the areas which provide opportunities for our representatives to develop a community feeling among all free peoples.

In portraying our vital role in the partnership of free peoples, it is appropriate to remind ourselves and our friends that we proceed from the strength of a notable history. It is the United States that constitutes the great revolutionary force of the modern era. It was in the Constitution of the United States that modern liberal thought found its flowering. From its earliest days, the United States has given strong support to other peoples who seek independence from overseas oppression or exploitation and who want to evolve their own ways of life. Millions of people are in charge of their own affairs today because of the powerful liberal influence of the United States. Our attachment to freedom is just as strong today as it was in earlier days. Our representation can do much to make this understood in the world. In the fog of propaganda and misunderstanding these fundamental facts are frequently forgotten.

This type of American representation abroad points to very heavy exactions upon our overseas personnel. In addition to their technical and professional equipment to handle the job, they should approach it with wide understanding. They should know American history and world history. They should be able to communicate with wide varieties of people. This may not necessarily require a knowledge of languages but it comes close to demanding it. Certainly there is a great need to develop languages among our representatives and our people generally if we are to be serious about filling a world leadership role.

We need regional as well as country experts. To obtain such men and women for our Foreign Service we must go to all strata of American society and choose persons who know the problems; we must not rely only on regular officials who are supposed to perform equally well wherever they are sent. In Germany, some of the finest public servants we had were men of German background who had come to the United States during the Hitler era. The knowledge of the local situation which these men had made them invaluable for our mission. Such men deserve a chance to remain in our Foreign Service.

Successful representation abroad is of crucial importance for this nation. For that reason our representatives should be held accountable. If men show they are failing in a mission, that they are not equipped to meet the situation, they should be removed. The time has passed when we can afford to keep men in posts who merely coast along until they weary of it, retire or are rotated in accordance with a sort of time-clock system. The conflict between the free nations and Soviet Russia is of such magnitude and scope that we cannot afford failure by lackadaisical effort at critical spots in the world. Our successful representatives abroad deserve full recognition and support. The others should make way for new men.

*   *   *   *   *

In this book emphasis has been put on the fact that the Soviet threat is all-inclusive and that the Soviets are employing a divisive technique to reach their goals. The answer to the Soviet threat lies in the growing development of multi-national institutions such as the European Coal and Steel Community, the European Defense Force, OEEC, NATO, ANZAS, and others.

These community projects must be a part of a greater undertaking, and that is the United Nations. For the United Nations, through all its vicissitudes, must be constantly projected as the community of all. We must hope and work to the end that some day the aggressive designs of the Kremlin will give way to more peaceful policies and actions, so that this institution will be able to perform its universal function.

The Soviet threat and the development of multi-national institutions to meet it place heavy responsibilities and new exactions on our government. Our military and civilian agencies have new roles to play and our State Department, in particular, must be invigorated by new ideas in policy-making at home and in policy-execution abroad. We can meet the challenge of the future if we make improvements where they are needed and if we steadfastly adhere to a concept of national interest which is based on law and morality.

Our postwar experience has demonstrated that the free nations must move together and that our efforts should be in the direction of cementing the relationships of the free peoples.

This is not a job for governments or diplomats alone. A large responsibility rests upon all of us to support the development of the communities of free nations in Europe, Asia, and in the rest of the world.

The universities carry a large share of this burden. They must train men and women to fill important jobs in Washington and around the world. They can make important contributions in identifying the problems of community and in developing answers in many areas. In this connection it may be observed that our intellectuals have not exerted the influence that they might have on the thinking abroad in regard to the significance of American political, economic and cultural developments. Many intellectuals abroad are adopting hostile attitudes which in some cases are merely poses and in others are the reflection of irritation over American influence. This would not be too disturbing if these European writers, thinkers and teachers did not preserve silence, both about what is going on in the United States in respect to our tremendous efforts to preserve a free society and what is going on in the Soviet Union and the satellite countries to suppress it. Where are the answers, for example, to some of the nonsense that Sartre has been currently writing? The American intellectual has not been vigorous and constructive in this field. He has been observant rather than active and consequently has not had the impact on thinking in Europe and in the rest of the world that he should have.

If the United States is to have effective representation abroad, all strata of our society must contribute to it. It is not solely the task of our official representatives for they need to be supported and armed with the thought and material which the nation as a whole, particularly our intellectuals, can bring to bear in the battle against freedom of the spirit. Not the least of the many dangers of irresponsible and one-sided investigative procedures is the fact that our intellectuals are so concerned over Congressional encroachments on free inquiry and personal rights that they may be in danger of ignoring the main threat to objective thought and action — the Communist threat.

Other institutions and organizations have large tasks to bear in these matters. Our private Foundations have the responsibility of supporting research, ideas and men, of providing means here and abroad to advance community projects which in turn would be advancing the cause of peace. Private and public organizations throughout the world have the duty of encouraging the interest and support of people. And the press and other information media, carrying the obligation of public enlightenment, should assume their share of the responsibility.

It is a lesson of American history that when we meet our responsibilities with minds open to new ideas and concepts, with determination, and with firm adherence to our tradition of tolerance and freedom, no challenge is too great for us. That is true today when we face the great challenges to our foreign policy, which are, in reality, challenges to peace and freedom in the world.

Date Due